OAK PARK PUBLIC LIB  W9-BCR-479

31132 012 562 637

OAK PARK PUBLIC LIBRARY

THE DUST BOWL

Essential Events

THE DUST
BOWL

BY SUE VANDER HOOK

Content Consultant
Dr. Pamela Riney-Kehrberg
Agricultural History and Rural Studies
Iowa State University

ABDO
Publishing Company

CREDITS

Published by ABDO Publishing Company, 8000 West 78th Street, Edina, Minnesota 55439. Copyright © 2009 by Abdo Consulting Group, Inc. International copyrights reserved in all countries. No part of this book may be reproduced in any form without written permission from the publisher. The Essential Library™ is a trademark and logo of ABDO Publishing Company.

Printed in the United States.

Editor: Jill Sherman
Copy Editor: Paula Lewis
Interior Design and Production: Emily Love
Cover Design: Emily Love

Library of Congress Cataloging-in-Publication Data
Vander Hook, Sue, 1949-
  The Dust Bowl / by Sue Vander Hook.
    p. cm. — (Essential events)
  Includes bibliographical references and index.
  ISBN 978-1-60453-512-9
  1. Dust Bowl Era, 1931-1939—Juvenile literature. 2. Great Plains—History—20th century—Juvenile literature. 3. Depressions—1929—Great Plains—Juvenile literature. 4. Droughts—Great Plains—History—20th century—Juvenile literature. 5. Agriculture—Great Plains—History—20th century—Juvenile literature. 6. Farmers—Great Plains—Social conditions—20th century—Juvenile literature. I. Title.
  F595.V26 2009
  978'.032—dc22

                                    2008033105

TABLE OF CONTENTS

Chapter 1	Black Sunday	6
Chapter 2	Prelude to Disaster	14
Chapter 3	Depression and Drought	24
Chapter 4	Farmers Fight Back	32
Chapter 5	Dusters, Snusters, and Black Blizzards	42
Chapter 6	Exodusters	56
Chapter 7	"Okie, Go Home!"	66
Chapter 8	Correcting the Okie Situation	76
Chapter 9	Healing the Land	88
Timeline		96
Essential Facts		100
Additional Resources		102
Glossary		104
Source Notes		106
Index		110
About the Author		112

A dust storm approaches Clayton, New Mexico.

BLACK SUNDAY

unday, April 14, 1935, dawned sunny and warm over the Great Plains. It had been months since the sky had been so blue and clear. Helen Wells, wife of the Methodist Episcopal minister in Guymon, Oklahoma, began cleaning the church early that morning. Dust flew into the air as she wiped off the pews, causing her to choke and cough, but by now she had grown accustomed to dust.

Her husband, the Reverend Rolley Wells, was preparing for a special "rain service." People were welcome to come to the church that morning to pray for rain and deliverance from a drought that was entering its fifth year. Two reporters from the *Saturday Evening Post* planned to attend. By midmorning, people arrived at the church in droves. Wells proclaimed, "Good rains within three weeks mean a harvest. God rules all and our last resort is prayer."[1]

When the service was over, families went outside to enjoy the rare dirt-free afternoon with picnics, road trips, and chores they had postponed for a day when the dust did not fly. The blue sky brought a ray of hope and optimism. By midafternoon, the temperature was 90 degrees Fahrenheit (32°C). But in just a few hours, the temperature suddenly dropped 50 degrees Fahrenheit (27.7°C). Huge flocks of ducks, geese, and smaller birds filled the sky, fluttering their wings in panic. Hordes of jackrabbits and other small animals scurried across the land.

THE BLACK BLIZZARD

Suddenly, on the northern horizon appeared an enormous dark cloud—commonly known as a black blizzard or a duster. This huge burst of wind and dirt rose thousands of feet into the air, energized by swirling 60-mile-per-hour (96.6-km/h) winds. It was not the first time a black blizzard had engulfed the plains. Large dust storms had plagued the region for four years.

The storm began in the Dakotas and eastern Wyoming. Strong, swirling winds picked up the dry topsoil and headed south through eastern Colorado and western Kansas. At 2:40 a.m. on April 14, 1935, just northeast of Guymon, the black blizzard struck Dodge City, Kansas. In the sudden darkness, some people thought the world was coming to an end. People took shelter if they could, and others caught in its path did their best to get home.

Types of Dust Storms

Dust storms range from insignificant "sand blows" to the "funnel storms" that sometimes lift dust thousands of feet into the air and carry it thousands of miles away. The Kansas Academy of Science has identified three classes of dust storms: rectilinear (moving in a straight line), rotational (revolving), and ebullition (sudden, violent outpouring).

SHELTER FROM THE STORM

Kansas farmer John Garretson and his wife Louise were in their car when they spotted the huge dark cloud. They tried to outrun it, but their car was soon engulfed in black dirt. Now on foot and blinded by the dust, they followed the fence wire hand over hand until they reached their home.

The storm moved on to the Oklahoma and Texas panhandles, hitting Guymon and nearby Boise City, Oklahoma, by late afternoon. Ed and Ada Phillips and their six-year-old daughter were driving home

The Great Plains

The Great Plains is a vast north-south stretch of prairie land and steppe east of the Rocky Mountains in Canada and the United States. The expanse covers parts of the Canadian provinces of Alberta, Saskatchewan, Manitoba, and British Columbia, and ten U.S. states—North Dakota, South Dakota, Nebraska, Kansas, Oklahoma, Texas, New Mexico, Colorado, Wyoming, and Montana.

The area periodically experiences years of drought. Typically, the region receives less than 20 inches (51 cm) of rainfall per year. Severe storms are common throughout the Great Plains states. Atmospheric pressures at Earth's surface clash and produce severe weather in the region. Air in a high-pressure system descends in a clockwise spiral, while air in a low-pressure system flows upward in a counterclockwise spiral. When the two systems meet, severe storms with high winds can result.

In the 1930s, these types of storms picked up dry topsoil and formed huge clouds of dirt and dust. The storms were called black blizzards or dusters. Later, many farms in the plains states began using irrigation systems to ensure water for their crops, especially in times of drought.

to Boise City. They were still 15 miles (24 km) away when the black blizzard appeared on the horizon. The Phillipses abandoned their vehicle and walked toward an old adobe house. On the way, the dust cloud hit them and everything turned black. Though unable to see, they managed to find the door to the two-room house. To their surprise, ten other people were inside, also seeking shelter. It was too dark to see each other's faces. But for the next four hours, they shared a common fear and a common shelter from the storm.

THE DUST BOWL

The next day, people across the plains tried to recover from the huge duster. They washed their dirt-caked faces, scooped buckets of dust from their homes, and dug out buried fences. Robert Geiger, an Associated Press reporter

"Little by little the sky was darkened by the mixing dust, and the wind felt over the earth, loosened the dust, and carried it away. The wind grew stronger. The rain crust broke and the dust lifted up out of the fields and drove gray plumes into the air like sluggish smoke. The corn threshed the wind and made a dry, rushing sound. The finest dust did not settle back to earth now, but disappeared into the darkening sky."[2]

—*John Steinbeck*, The Grapes of Wrath

Dust and topsoil are picked up by strong winds.

for the *Washington Evening Star*, had been traveling through Guymon on Black Sunday. On Monday, he wrote the first of three articles about the storms that were ravaging the Great Plains. In his first article, he referred to "life in the dust bowl of the continent."[3] Thus, the Dust Bowl got its name. The public immediately adopted the term that so aptly described the Great Plains disaster of the 1930s. Other journalists across the country also reported the events of Black Sunday, which would be the most

The Great Plains was plagued by dust storms in the 1930s, but other extremes also afflicted the area during that period. Tornadoes often hit the area, and temperatures surpassed 120 degrees Fahrenheit (49°C). Mixtures of dirt and snow reached blizzard proportions in what were called snusters, and an earthquake shook the ground in 1936. The years 1934 to 1936 were record drought years for the entire United States.

devastating storm of the Dust Bowl era. In an article for *The New Republic*, Avis Carlson wrote:

> *The impact is like a shovelful of fine sand flung against the face. People caught in their own yards grope for the doorstep. Cars come to a standstill, for no light in the world can penetrate that swirling murk. . . . We live with the dust, eat it, sleep with it, watch it strip us of possessions and the hope of possessions.*[4]

The Dust Bowl era lasted throughout the 1930s. It eventually picked up approximately 10 billion tons (9 billion t) of topsoil from the Great Plains and dumped it along its eastward path across the United States. The storms scattered dust and dirt on Chicago, Illinois, and cities as far east as New York City, finally depositing dirt into the Atlantic Ocean. The Dust Bowl was the United States' greatest environmental catastrophe. It delivered widespread economic and agricultural damage across the entire country.

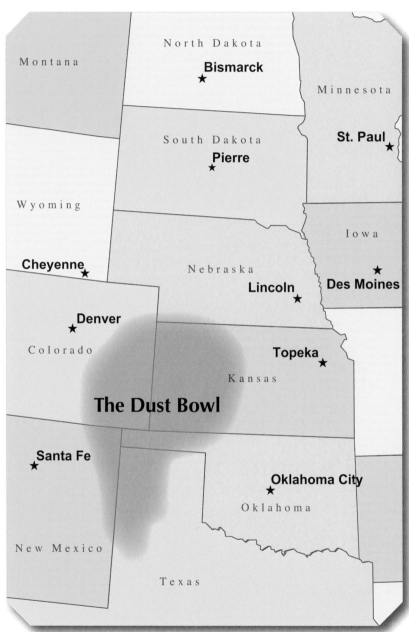

Most of the Great Plains was affected by dust storms and drought. The actual Dust Bowl was located in parts of Colorado, Kansas, Nebraska, New Mexico, Oklahoma, and Texas.

The Chrisman sisters built their homesteads on the Great Plains in the late 1800s.

PRELUDE TO DISASTER

xtreme weather was not a new phenomenon in the Great Plains. This area was hit with winter blizzards, powerful, unpredictable winds, and dry summers that cracked the soil. Yet, the land had been resilient. It survived the droughts and winds that repeatedly swirled dust over the region.

The vegetation always recovered after the wind and the heat. It even withstood the regular assaults by millions of swarming locusts, which ate everything in their path. The tall grass grew back, and the trees along the riverbanks survived. Sometimes, lightning struck patches of dry prairie grass, igniting blazes that blackened millions of acres. The winds would pick up the ashes and dust and drop them over entire regions. Drought, wind, locusts, and fire were all natural events on the plains, but the land always recovered. Often the soil was nourished by these natural phenomena. When thick, dry grass was destroyed by fire, the soil was able to absorb more water and nutrients, causing broad-bladed grass to grow back even thicker. The dense prairie grass and wildflowers anchored the topsoil and shielded it against forceful winds.

Prairie Grass

Before the U.S. prairie lands were settled, native grasslands covered approximately two-thirds of the region. The three prominent grasses were Big Bluestem, Indian grass, and Prairie Cord grass. These grasses could grow as tall as 9 feet (2.7 m). Across the prairie, there were about 150 types of grasses, including Little Bluestem, Prairie Dropseed, Porcupine grass, and Needlegrass. Prior to the 1930s, few farmers understood how important these grasses were for the preservation of the soil.

HISTORY OF THE PLAINS

Native American tribes such as Blackfeet, Cheyenne, Comanche, and Pawnee once inhabited the plains. They lived in traditional tepees, hunted bison on the open range, and planted gardens on the river's edge. Europeans began arriving in the Great Plains in the mid-sixteenth century. The fur trade attracted trappers from Spain, France, England, Russia, and parts of North America.

In 1803, the United States purchased 530 million acres

The Louisiana Purchase

Spain once controlled the Louisiana Territory. The United States had a 1795 treaty with Spain that gave Americans access to New Orleans to ship goods such as tobacco, flour, pork, lard, and dairy products. Spain revoked its treaty with the United States in 1798 and transferred the Louisiana Territory to France in a secret treaty in 1800.

Rumors of the secret treaty reached the United States. President Thomas Jefferson wanted to ensure Americans had access to the Mississippi River and the port of New Orleans. Jefferson was prepared to spend $10 million for New Orleans alone; but the price of the entire Louisiana Territory was only $15 million and it included New Orleans.

The full size of the Louisiana Territory was unknown. Even before the Louisiana Purchase was completed, plans were made to send explorers to the area. Meriwether Lewis and William Clark charted the territory and explored the region from 1804 to 1806. The land of the Louisiana Purchase covers about 23 percent of the present-day United States, approximately 828,000 square miles (2,144,520 sq km). The land purchase opened up the way for more American traders and settlers to go West.

(214 million ha) of North American land from
France for $15 million, or about four cents per
acre (7 cents per ha). It was called the Louisiana
Purchase. The area included many present-day Great
Plains states and opened the way for the United
States to expand farther west. During the nineteenth
century, explorers, trappers, and missionaries came
in greater numbers to the plains and learned to cope
with the area's extreme weather.

Newspapers reported on the region's strong
storms and fires. In 1855, an editor wrote:

> *Our houses are all open, and the wind whistles in at every*
> *crevice, bringing along with it a heavy load of fine particles*
> *of charcoal, ashes, etc., and depositing it on our type, paper,*
> *library, furniture, and in fact not regarding our dinner, but*
> *liberally covering it with condiment for which we have no*
> *relish.*[1]

A storm on April 3, 1860, was particularly brutal.
The editor of the *Fort Scott Democrat* in Kansas reported
that the dust storm was "by far the most disagreeable
we ever experienced. For the space of half an hour
the cloud of dust was so intense that it was impossible
to distinguish objects at the distance of a dozen
yards."[2]

"Free Land!"

Despite the extreme weather conditions in the plains, many Americans were drawn to the area. They were attracted by the vast open spaces of the Western frontier. In 1862, during the American Civil War (1861–1865), President Abraham Lincoln signed the Homestead Act. This act granted land in the West to settlers who met certain requirements. A person had to be at least 21 years old and either a U.S. citizen or intending to become a U.S. citizen; the person could not have fought against the United States or given aid to its enemies. A qualified person had to file an application with the Land Office for ten dollars. The applicant also had to sign a statement saying that he or she would build a house on the land and live there for at least five years. The maximum land grant was 160 acres (65 ha) for an individual and 320 acres (129.5 ha) for a couple.

"Free Land!" became the cry of thousands who eagerly headed west on horseback, in wagons, or on foot to claim their acreage. Land runs, as they were called, helped settle many areas of the plains throughout the nineteenth century. Approximately 50,000 people lined up at noon on April 22, 1889, to make a rush for their piece of the 2 million acres

Homesteaders gather to make their claims on August 6, 1901.

(810,000 ha) offered by the U.S. government. In just one day, two cities—Oklahoma City and Guthrie—were established with approximately 10,000 people each. The May 18, 1889, edition of *Harpers Weekly* reported:

> Unlike Rome, the city of Guthrie was built in a day. To be strictly accurate in the matter, it might be said that it was built in an afternoon. At twelve o'clock on Monday, April 22d, the resident population of Guthrie was nothing; before sundown it was at least ten thousand. In that time streets had

been laid out, town lots staked off, and steps taken toward the formation of a municipal government. . . . Never before in the history of the West has so large a number of people been concentrated in one place in so short a time.[3]

For the rest of the century, an onslaught of pioneers settled the West. Many arrived in covered wagons, claimed their land, built their homes, and established ranches and farms.

AMERICA'S BREADBASKET

By 1910, nearly 1 million acres (404,686 ha) of land were planted, mostly in wheat, which grew well in the soil. Farmers also planted corn, oats, barley, rye, and sorghum.

As better farm equipment became available, farmers could plow more land and plant more crops in less time with fewer hired hands. When gas tractors came into use in about 1910, farming boomed. Great Plains farmers were especially successful during World War I (1914–1918). Because many European farmers had left their fields to fight the war, crop production declined in Europe—increasing the demand for American wheat. "Wheat will win the war!" was a common wartime slogan. From 1910 to 1920, land planted in wheat alone increased from 466,000 acres (188,583 ha) to almost 1.2 million acres (485,622 ha). Total U.S. cropland increased to nearly 2.3 million acres (930,776 ha). The price of wheat more than doubled, soaring from ninety-one cents per bushel to more than two dollars.

High wheat prices encouraged farmers to plant more crops and purchase more farm equipment. Every year, farmers were tilling more soil, planting more crops, and harvesting faster. It was easy for farmers to borrow money to purchase the latest equipment; banks were eager to extend credit during such prosperous times.

Wheat farming was so profitable that people who lived hundreds of miles away and had other jobs purchased farmland in the Great Plains. These "suitcase farmers," as they were called, bought up thousands of acres and hired farmers to cultivate, plant, and harvest their land. If drought destroyed the crops, the landowners let the land sit barren. Farming was not their main source of income. But when the land was bare, extreme weather took its toll on the unprotected soil.

Farming Practices

Poor farming practices also damaged the land. Some farmers burned the stubble that remained after a wheat harvest; others grazed their cattle in the stalk fields until every bit of vegetation was devoured. Deep tilling exposed more soil and destroyed prairie grass roots. This left the land unprotected from the inevitable drought, wind, and fires. But successful farmers thought the rain and the harvests would continue. Melt White, son of a Texas farmer, said:

> *It looked like it was just a thing that would never end. So they abused the land; they abused it something terrible . . . we don't even think what the end results might be.*[4]

Wheat prices dropped dramatically during the 1920s, but farmers offset the low prices by tilling more land, planting more crops, and buying more tractors to get the job done quickly. Many farmers ran their tractors all day and night. The weather cooperated and farmers prospered.

But at the end of the 1920s, the profits and the wealth came to an abrupt halt. The Roaring Twenties were over, and what followed would be called the Great Depression, the Dirty Thirties, and the Dust Bowl.

The Great Plains was known as America's breadbasket for
its production of wheat.

Investors gather on Wall Street following the stock market crash of 1929.

DEPRESSION AND
DROUGHT

On October 24, 1929, an infamous day known as Black Thursday, stock prices fell at an alarming rate. Five days later, on October 29—Black Tuesday—stock prices plunged even further. People who had invested in stocks now rushed to sell them before prices dipped more. Although not everyone was directly hurt by the market crash, its effects began to spread across the country. Many Americans became aware that the economy was fragile and prosperity would not last forever.

Very few people were actually wealthy during the 1920s, and after the crash they were unable to repay their creditors. By the 1930s, the nation was in the midst of an economic disaster that would be known as the Great Depression. Many Americans withdrew all their money from their banks and virtually stopped spending. Factories that had produced thousands of washing machines, refrigerators, and automobiles slowed down production. Employees lost their jobs. Some factories shut their doors and stopped production completely. More and more people found themselves jobless and deeply in debt.

For many farmers, their troubles had begun well before the market crash. On November 9, 1929, Ann Marie Low wrote in her diary,

> There seems to be quite a furor in the country over a big stock market crash that wiped a lot of people out. We are ahead

of them. The hailstorm in July of 1928 and bank failure
that fall wiped out a lot of people locally. [1]

The Great Depression

The Great Depression lasted from 1929 until 1941, when the United States entered World War II. Although it was primarily an American economic collapse, the Depression affected most of the world's industrialized countries, which had become economically dependent on each other.

The worst conditions during the Depression were in the farming, mining, and logging communities. The hardest hit commodities, or products, were wheat, cotton, tobacco, and lumber. Prices plunged and unemployment soared. American industries halted the large-scale production that had characterized the 1920s.

Blame for the Depression varied. Some people believed it was the collapse of capitalism, or privately owned businesses. Others believed big business had too much power. Some blamed the banking industry for allowing unwise loans.

President Herbert Hoover implemented some programs to relieve the effects of the Depression. However, Hoover believed the government should not play too large a role. He felt that Americans should help themselves and help each other through volunteerism. Many Americans blamed Hoover for not doing enough to end the Depression.

Indeed, crop prices had begun to drop throughout the 1920s. Now, crop prices fell as much as 60 percent. Farmers tried to compensate for the low prices by planting more crops, but the fields yielded more than they could sell. American crops were no longer in demand in Europe and so the U.S. market was flooded with wheat that could not fetch a decent price. Surpluses piled up and prices fell even further. The farmers' suffering was multiplied by the extremely harsh weather conditions that ravaged the land.

DROUGHT HITS THE GREAT PLAINS

Between 1929 and 1931, wheat prices fell from about one dollar a bushel to thirty-four cents. Hail, drought, heat, and fires plagued the Great Plains early in the decade. In 1930, hail destroyed Caroline and Wilhelmine Henderson's wheat crop near Shelton, Oklahoma. In 1931, they produced a good crop, but by then the price of wheat had bottomed out. In the summer of 1931, the rain stopped, and the Hendersons barely survived.

That summer, the heat and drought had nearly destroyed all the crops on Ann Marie Low's North Dakota farm. She wrote in her diary on June 30:

> It is so hot! Dad's flax just cooked in the ground. It is all gone. Fields and pastures are burned brown.

> The heat deaths . . . total 1,231. I mean humans. Lord only knows how many

Flax

Flax is harvested for its seed as well as its fibers. Flax seeds are used to make linseed or flaxseed oils. For centuries, processed flaxseed oil has been used in paints and varnishes. Its uses vary from making fabric and paper to producing soap, dye, and medicines. Some people plant flax for its decorative flowers.

animals have died. Scotts recently lost their dog and a cow to the heat. Cattle are starving all over the state, and there is no market for them. Horses drop dead in the fields from the heat. The milk cows have so little to eat they are going dry. People pasture their grain fields and then plow them up to conserve moisture for next year—if moisture comes.[2]

From 1931 to 1935, drought destroyed bumper wheat crops and left cattle and sheep to die from starvation and dehydration. The severe four-year drought took its worst toll on parts of Colorado, Kansas, Oklahoma, and Texas. This land would be called the Dust Bowl. Rainfall in these states ranged from 3 to 9 inches (7.6 to 22.9 cm). This was well below the typical 18 inches (45.7 cm). Since every drop of rain was critical for healthy crops, even a few inches below average resulted in crop damage.

Scorched Land

During the 1930s, scarcely anything grew on the scorched land. But each year, farmers continued to till and plant the soil, hoping that the next crop would thrive.

The drought persisted and record summer temperatures reached 120 degrees Fahrenheit

(49°C) in some places. Any grain that managed to sprout was dried up by the heat. Kansas farmer Lawrence Svobida recalled:

I had planted wheat in 1929, in 1930, and in 1931. I had planted barley and I had planted maize. I had planted five crops and harvested only one, for which I had received a miserably low price. You might have thought I would have become convinced that there was no profit in farming wheat in the Great Plains. But I was a glutton for punishment, and here I was planting wheat again, and still hoping.[3]

In the scorching summer heat, much of the land lay abandoned with either tilled soil or stubbles of wheat that had not survived the dryness. Hungry cattle grazed among the stubbles and ate the failed wheat crop, roots and all, exposing even more dry soil.

Dust storms were inevitable. The people of the plains were accustomed to billowing dust, but they were overwhelmed by the massive storms of the 1930s. In January 1932, a duster with winds

Hailstorms

In July 1928, a severe hailstorm hit North Dakota and wiped out acres of crops. A damaging hailstorm also hit Potter, Nebraska, the same month. The Nebraska storm produced a hailstone that measured 17.2 inches (43.7 cm) in circumference and weighed 1.51 pounds (0.68 kg). It was the largest hailstone on record until September 3, 1970, when a storm in Coffeyville, Kansas, produced a hailstone measuring 17.5 inches (44.5 cm) and weighing 1.67 pounds (0.76 kg).

up to 60 miles per hour (96.6 km/h) picked up loose dirt and rolled upward as high as 10,000 feet (3,048 m) before it hit Amarillo, Texas. It continued on its destructive path to Oklahoma and Kansas, damaging homes, businesses, and crops on its way.

But not all farmers quietly waited for conditions to improve. One group of farmers not only voiced their protests, but they also took action.

Without rain, soil can dry up and crack.

When farmers could not pay their bills, banks seized their property and sold it at farm auctions.

FARMERS FIGHT BACK

In 1932, a group of Iowa farmers fought back against the incredibly low prices offered for their milk and produce. They wanted all farmers to unite and refuse to deliver their products to market—they wanted to strike. They believed that if the supply went down, prices would go up.

Some farmers did unite. On May 3, 1932, at a convention of Iowa farmers, 3,000 farmers led by Milo Reno voted to strike on July 4. Their slogan was "Stay at Home—Buy Nothing, Sell Nothing." Thousands of farmers refused to send their produce to market unless they were paid at least what it cost them to plant and harvest the crops.

Not all farmers participated in the strike, and protesting farmers took action. They blocked roads to stop farmers who were not on strike from delivering their milk and cream to market. When these farmers refused to turn their trucks around, the strikers dumped their milk onto the road. With pitchforks and rakes in hand, the strikers threatened anyone who dared to cross the barricade. Some hurled rocks through farm-truck windshields, beat up drivers, and dumped produce and wheat on the ground. Police broke up the skirmishes and opened the roads. The strikes had no effect on the market.

Milo Reno

Milo Reno joined the Iowa Farmers Union in 1918. By 1921, he was president of the organization. Reno worked to make the union into a successful organization that included stores, gas stations, and insurance companies— all for the benefit of farmers. He believed if farmers united, they could build a strong corporation that would raise the status of the American farmer.

FORECLOSURES AND AUCTIONS

The price for wheat and other crops continued to drop, incomes plummeted, and loans and mortgages became overdue. Farmers had taken out large loans to purchase land and farm equipment; they also had mortgages on their houses and barns. When a farmer could not make his payments, the bank that held title to the land got a court order to sell the farm at public auction. The farm went to the highest bidder, and the bank got some or all of its money back. In 1932, banks foreclosed on approximately 1,000 farms a week.

Make It Rain

In Dalhart, Texas, explosive expert Tex Thornton told a group of local residents that setting off dynamite in the air could bring rain. Farmers and ranchers gave Thornton $300 to purchase explosives and send them up in balloons into low-lying clouds. However, an unexpected dust storm thwarted their plans. It was too windy to send the explosives into the air, so Thornton buried 60 charges in the sand and lit the fuses. The explosions sent dirt flying into the air, where it mixed with the already-swirling dust storm. No rain fell on Dalhart that evening.

Some farmers retaliated and threatened to destroy their farms before the banks could take them. One farmer vowed:

> If they come to take my farm, I'm going to fight. I'd rather be killed outright than die by starvation. But before I die, I'm going to set fire to my crops. I'm going to burn my house! I'm going to p'izen [poison] my cattle.[1]

Other farmers rigged the auction process in what came to be called "penny auctions" or "Sears Roebuck sales."
The first penny auction took place in Iowa in 1931 and quickly caught on. A group of farmers would attend an auction and not allow anyone else to bid. Sometimes by threat and other times by force, these farmers controlled the bidding. A dangling noose in clear sight of all who attended became the mark that identified these special sales. The farmers would bid a few pennies or

"This Land Is Your Land"

Woody Guthrie was in his twenties during the Dust Bowl era. Through guitar-accompanied ballads, Guthrie told stories of a broken, demoralized people from the Dust Bowl. Guthrie's ballad, "This Land Is Your Land," has become an American standard:

This land is your land. This land is my land
From California to the New York island;
From the redwood forest to the Gulf Stream waters
This land was made for you and me.

As I was walking that ribbon of highway,
I saw above me that endless skyway:
I saw below me that golden valley:
This land was made for you and me.

I've roamed and rambled and followed my footsteps
To the sparkling sands of her diamond deserts;
And all around me a voice was sounding:
This land was made for you and me.

When the sun came shining, and I was strolling,
And the wheat fields waving and the dust clouds rolling,
As the fog was lifting a voice was chanting:
This land was made for you and me.[2]

several dollars on farm equipment or the farm, and then no one else dared offer a bid. The auctioneer's attempts to raise the bid were met with silence and snickering, and he was forced to announce that the item was sold to the highest bidder. The new owner then returned the item to the original owner, who was now free of debt.

A New Deal for Farmers

The penny auctions and strikes eventually got the attention of Congress. President Franklin D. Roosevelt took office in March 1933. He immediately went to work to deal with the Depression. In the 100 days that followed Roosevelt's inauguration, Congress passed rapid-fire legislation to help relieve the dreadful economic state of the country. One new piece of legislation was the Agricultural Adjustment Act (AAA), which allowed the government to give financial aid to farmers who agreed to leave some of their fields unplanted. The less that was produced, the higher the prices would be, and farmers would eventually benefit.

The newly formed Agricultural Adjustment Administration, in charge of distributing subsidies, went to work that year after farmers had planted

A resettlement administrator inspects the parched soil.

their fields. In order to reduce surpluses, the agency carried out a large-scale destruction of crops. In addition, livestock were slaughtered to raise the price of pork and beef. Most Americans were angered by the destruction of produce and meat during a time when so many people were starving. But within three years, the government's plan was working—farm prices went up, and farmers' incomes increased.

The AAA was one of many laws that were part of Roosevelt's New Deal. His plan was to provide relief, recovery, and reform—the three Rs—to the poor and unemployed people of the United States. When Roosevelt took office, 25 percent of the American people were unemployed. It had become a way of life in the United States. In nearly every American city, jobless men waited in long lines outside homeless shelters every day hoping for a place to eat and sleep. Unable to find work, approximately 250,000 teenagers roamed the country aimlessly "riding the rails."

Agricultural Adjustment Act

In 1936, the U.S. Supreme Court declared the Agricultural Adjustment Act (AAA) unconstitutional. The Court determined that the AAA did not delegate taxes fairly. The AAA was replaced by a similar program. Since then, federal regulation of agriculture has been revised many times. Farm subsidies are still in effect today.

They hopped aboard freight trains and bummed food along the way. Some left home to ease their family's burden and give them one less mouth to feed. Others were looking for adventure, jobs, or a better life.

THE HOMELESS

From New York City to Seattle, Washington, the homeless made do—they built shanties out of boxes, old metal, tar paper, or scraps of wood. Shanties were often lined up side by side for miles in what came to be called Hoovervilles—after President Herbert Hoover. Many believed Hoover could have done more to help the American people during the Depression. Belle Weight was eight years old when she saw her first Hooverville in Seattle:

> As we rode along the Seattle waterfront we passed about a hundred shanties built from pieces of scrap metal and packing crates. The tenants were huddled around small bonfires as the perpetual Puget Sound rain drizzled down. . . . Herbert Hoover had wanted a chicken in every pot but these people didn't even have a pot, cooking or otherwise.[3]

People who held Hoover in contempt now embraced Roosevelt, who promised, "I pledge you, I pledge myself, to a new deal for the American people."[4] Many New Deal laws addressed the needs of farmers and resulted in agencies such as the Resettlement Administration (RA), which was later called the Farm Security Administration. This agency provided government funds to resettle farmers to more productive farms.

Some farmers also took advantage of programs directed at the general population, such as the Civilian Conservation Corps (CCC), which provided work for young men in construction and in the nation's forests planting trees and fighting fires. Eventually, the CCC put 2.5 million men back to work. Other people worked for the Works Progress Administration (WPA), a federal program that hired people to build public buildings, dams, bridges, roads, and other public facilities.

But federal aid would not be enough for many farmers in the plains states. Dust storms damaged the crops to such an extent that recovery seemed impossible. In 1933, wind gales were stronger than usual, and dust storms became more frequent and forceful. Goodwell, Oklahoma, recorded 30 dust storms in the first seven months of 1933. Caroline Henderson recalled:

> There are days when for hours at a time we cannot see the windmill fifty feet from the kitchen door. There are days when for briefer periods one cannot distinguish the windows from the solid wall because of the solid blackness of the raging storm.[5]

For most of the 1930s dust storms caused destruction across the plains states.

Dust storms added to farmers' troubles following the extended drought.

Women cover their faces from the dust as they pump water during a storm.

Dusters, Snusters, and Black Blizzards

ortions of Colorado, Kansas, Oklahoma, and Texas were the worst hit by dust storms. Dusters turned sunshine into a dark haze and forced people to use lights in the middle of the afternoon. Through the plumes of dust, sunlight cast everything in a purple or green tint. Motorists had to use their headlights to find their way through the dust storms and around huge sand drifts that blew across the roads. Strong static electricity from the storms sometimes stalled cars or caused them to not run at all. Anything made of metal—cooking pans, barbed wire, water-pump handles, doorknobs—became highly charged with electricity, giving a static shock to anyone who touched them.

Young J. R. Davison from Texas later described the dusters:

We could see this low cloud bank it looked like. You could see it all the way across. And we watched that thing and it got closer. Seemed to kind of grow you know and it was getting closer. The ends of it would seem to sweep around. And you felt like you know you were surrounded. Finally, it would just close in on you. Shut off all the light. You couldn't see a thing.[1]

Melt White later recalled:

And it kept getting worse and worse. And the wind kept blowing harder and harder. It kept getting darker and darker. And the old house is just a-vibratin' like it was gonna blow away. And I started trying to see my hand. And I kept bringing my hand up closer and closer and closer and closer. And I finally touched the end of my nose and I still couldn't see my hand. That's how black it was. A lot of people got out of bed, got their children out of the bed. Got down praying, thought that was it. They thought that was the end of the world. [2]

People usually had some warning of an approaching dust storm. The wind blew harder, and birds and small animals raced by in search of shelter. Seeing this, farm families would herd cows into their barns, secure farm equipment, stuff cracks with wet towels, and take cover.

Winter weather could also bring brutal storms and sometimes shut down businesses and schools for days. When winds were strong enough, they picked up topsoil and mixed it with snow in the air, creating cold, dirty blizzards called snusters. This dirty snow often traveled eastward, dumping the filthy snow in cities such as Chicago, Illinois, and Boston, Massachusetts.

Black Blizzards

Large dust storms that carried tons of black dirt were called black blizzards. They grew in strength and size as they roared across the land picking up tons of parched topsoil. Winds were so strong that

A dust storm approaches Springfield, Colorado.

the blowing dirt could strip the paint off the side of a house. Visibility was often less than 50 feet (15 m) and sometimes less than one foot (0.3 m) when a duster hit. People caught outside had to cover their faces with handkerchiefs or towels in order to breathe. Then they could only hope that they found their way home in the utter darkness.

A resident of Beadle County, South Dakota, described a storm that hit on November 11, 1933:

> By mid-morning, a gale was blowing, cold and black. By noon it was blacker than night, because one can see through

A mother and her son in their Dust Bowl farmhouse

night and this was an opaque black. It was a wall of dirt one's eyes could not penetrate. . . . When the wind died and the sun shone forth again, it was on a different world. There were no fields, only sand drifting into mounds and eddies that swirled in what was now but an autumn breeze.[3]

Schools sent students home early when a dust storm was on the horizon. Children needed time to get home safely before a black blizzard struck. When storms hit without warning, students and teachers stayed at school and studied by the light of lanterns. Sometimes they stayed all night until the wind calmed.

The fine dust always found its way inside houses and buildings. When people spotted a duster, they quickly stuffed rags in the cracks around their doors and draped oil-soaked towels over their windows in hopes that the wet substance would trap the dust. But the dust sifted through the crevices and deposited one inch (2.5 cm) or more on floors, beds, tables, chairs, dishes, and food. People began to store flour in tight-lidded jars and cover fresh-baked pies with towels. At night, families slept with wet cloths or sponges over their faces to filter the dust. But in the morning, their hair was caked with dirt, and their tongues and teeth were covered with grit.

Destruction Left Behind

Cleanup after a storm was hard work. Family members grabbed brooms and swept the dust and dirt into piles, choking on the gritty air as they worked. They sometimes used shovels to scoop up piles of dirt and then deposited the powdery substance outside, where mounds and drifts of sand were heaped high.

Outside, tumbleweeds stuck to fences and were covered by mounds of dust. Farmers usually left the fences buried rather than dig them out repeatedly. Typically, after a storm farmers had to dig out the barn door and give fresh water to the animals. Sometimes chickens, dogs, pigs, and even cattle had to be dug out of drifts. Children had to clean the dirt out of the cows' nostrils. Nothing could be done to repair the crop damage. Crops were either ripped out of the ground or smothered and buried.

These huge dust storms made newspaper headlines across the country. Reporters described the thick darkness, ruined crops, traffic brought to a standstill, and dying animals whose stomachs were filled with "mud balls" from eating dust-covered food. Animals also suffocated from dust in their lungs. Dust-related health problems were common in the Dust Bowl. Dust pneumonia caused inflamed lungs from breathing in too much dirt. Hospitals were overwhelmed with cases of the disease, and parents warned their children about the dangers of breathing in too much dust.

Dust was not the only problem in the 1930s. Food was scarce, and farmers turned to hunting jackrabbits for food. A typical Dust Bowl meal was beans, biscuits, and "fried jack." As each drought year passed, the food supply lessened.

Storms Continue

In April 1934, Kansas rainfall was less than it had been in 24 years. Most of western Kansas received less than 0.5 inches (1.3 cm) of rain. That month, a huge black blizzard hit Baca County in southeastern Colorado, blasting powdery dust into the air with winds of 50 miles per hour (80.5 km/h). Dust shrouded the sun for six days. Dust storms hit other states such as North Dakota that month as well. Ann Marie Low wrote in her diary:

April 25, 1934, Wednesday. Last weekend was the worst dust storm we ever had. We've been having quite a bit of blowing dirt every year since the drouth [drought] started, not only here, but all over the Great Plains. Many days this spring the air is just full of dirt coming, literally for hundreds of miles. It sifts into everything. After we wash the dishes and put them away, so much dirt sifts

Health Problems

Dust storms caused many health hazards, including sinusitis, pharyngitis, laryngitis, bronchitis, and pneumonia. The very young and the very old were at greatest risk of respiratory illnesses caused by fine particles of dust in the lungs.

Respiratory and other health problems became so bad in Guymon, Oklahoma, that residents turned church basements into emergency hospitals. In eastern Colorado, during the first few months of 1935, dust storms were responsible for six deaths, more than 100 serious illnesses, and thousands of dead jackrabbits and livestock.

into the cupboards we must wash them again before the next meal. Clothes in the closets are covered with dust. Last weekend no one was taking an automobile out for fear of ruining the motor. I rode Roany to Frank's place to return a gear. To find my way I had to ride right beside the fence, scarcely able to see from one fence post to the next. Newspapers say the deaths of many babies and old people are attributed to breathing in so much dirt.[4]

In May 1934, an enormous dust cloud emerged, stretching 1,500 miles (2,414 km) long and 900 miles (1,448 km) wide. For 36 hours,

"Dust Pneumonia Blues"

Folksinger Woody Guthrie's song about dust pneumonia portrayed the sometimes deadly disease that was unique to the Dust Bowl:

"Dust Pneumonia Blues"

I got that dust pneumony, pneumony in my lung,
I got the dust pneumony, pneumony in my lung,
An' I'm a-gonna sing this dust pneumony song.

I went to the doctor, and the doctor, said, "My son,"
I went to the doctor, and the doctor, said, "My son,
You got that dust pneumony an' you ain't got long, not long."

Now there ought to be some yodelin' in this song;
Yeah, there ought to be some yodelin' in this song;
But I can't yodel for the rattlin' in my lung.

My good gal sings the dust pneumony blues.
My good gal sings the dust pneumony blues,
She loves me 'cause she's got the dust pneumony, too.[5]

winds lifted 350 million tons (318 million t) of dirt
into the air. The storm dumped 12 million tons
(11 million t) of dust on Chicago, Illinois. Dust
reached cities as far away as Buffalo, New York,
Boston, Massachusetts, and Atlanta, Georgia. The
storm finally rolled out over the Atlantic Ocean,
where ships 300 miles (483 km) out were sprinkled
with dust. There was no way to predict when a storm
would hit, how long it would last, or how far it would
travel. As severe as the storms were in 1934, however,
the worst storms were yet to come in 1935.

On February 21, 1935, a huge duster hit western
Kansas, Oklahoma, and Texas. Traffic halted,
schools closed, and sports events were cancelled.
One Kansas farmer did not make it home that
day. He suffocated on the dust halfway between his
abandoned car and his house. Amarillo, Texas, was
draped in dust for 28 days. Dodge City, Kansas, was
covered with dust for 26 days. In Dighton, Kansas, a
train engineer was unable to see the warning signals
through the dust and rammed a passenger train.
Thirty-two people were injured in the accident.

Trains could barely move along the tracks, and
someone had to walk ahead to determine if drifts
were high enough to derail the train. Crewmen had

to shovel sand off the tracks. Sometimes snowplows were brought in to clear the rails.

On April 14, 1935, Dust Bowl residents experienced the worst duster they had ever seen. The storm began in the Dakotas and roared through Wyoming, eastern Colorado, western Kansas, and the Oklahoma and Texas panhandles. Wanita Brown of Amarillo, Texas, described the haunting experience:

> And the dust was just rolling in, just like a fog coming in, and in no time it was as dark as night. Yes, I remember that day. You know, we couldn't imagine whether the world was coming to an end or what.[6]

The day that storm hit would later be called Black Sunday. The storm was the most devastating to hit the area during the Dust Bowl era.

CONTINUED OPTIMISM

Even in the face of some of the worst dust storms, farmers were not willing to go down without a fight. Some continued to plan confidently for the future, under the assumption that rains would eventually come. Imogene Glover told of her father's endless hope:

My daddy was an optimist. I think he just kept thinking, "Next year will be better and we'll have a good crop and we'll raise some more cattle and we'll get rich." We never did, but he thought we would. . . . He really believed that everything would work out for the best, that we'd have a good crop and—and everything would be better.[7]

Newspaper editor John McCarty took on the challenge of encouraging farmers to stay on the land and not give up. McCarty pledged to stay in the plains, even if he was the last man standing, and he dared others to do the same. When about a hundred people stepped up to the challenge, the Last Man's Club was formed. Every member promised:

In the absence of an act of God, serious family injury, or some other emergency, I pledge to stay here as the last man and to do everything I can to help other last men remain in this country. We promise to stay here 'til hell freezes over and skate out on the ice.[10]

Keeping Spirits Up

In the midst of the Dust Bowl disaster, many people kept a keen sense of humor. John L. McCarty, editor of the *Dalhart Texan*, brought wit and absurdity to the predicament. He encouraged Texans caught in the Dust Bowl to "[g]rab a root and growl."[8] In an article titled "A Tribute to Our Sandstorms," McCarty described the beauty of a black blizzard with its purple, blue, and dark green colors enhanced by a dark blue sky and rays of sunlight. He and a friend lightheartedly planned to build a hotel in the middle of the sand drifts, attracting tourists to experience the "noble grandeur and imposing beauty of a Panhandle sandstorm."[9]

Some farmers were reluctant to accept government aid. However, most had no choice in the matter. Farmers took advantage of government assistance plans in order to stay. But Lawrence Svobida realized "anything the Government can do makes only a dent in a problem so vast that it staggers the intellect and even the imagination of man."[11]

Children were especially prone to respiratory illness in the Dust Bowl.

A family of migrants change a tire on their way to California.

EXODUSTERS

hree-fourths of Dust Bowlers stayed in
the Great Plains, persevering through the
Depression and drought. Lawrence Svobida decided
to stay, saying, "I came to the conclusion that the
only crop I had left was the wheat in the lone quarter
section that had held . . . but I could not bring

myself to leave my farm so long as I had that one quarter of wheat."[1]

By 1935, however, after four years of drought, blistering heat, prairie fires, failed crops, and ever-growing black blizzards, millions of people began leaving the Dust Bowl. They were either "blown out," "burned out," or "starved out" of the land they still loved.

Land Destroyed

In 1934, a federal report estimated that 35 million arable acres (14.2 million ha) had been destroyed in the Dust Bowl and nearly all the topsoil of another 125 million acres (50.6 million ha) had eroded. Serious damage was in progress on yet another 100 million acres (40.5 million ha).

At the same time as Dust Bowlers were giving up on their farms, tenant farmers were losing their jobs as well. Jobs were eliminated by labor-saving tractors and farm equipment. Tractors reduced the need for human labor and eliminated many tenant farm families. Landowners were now farming their own land. In some cases, loan companies and banks owned the land they had foreclosed on and hired one man to run a large tractor.

People wrote letters to newspapers and members of Congress. A letter to the *Dallas Farm News* read:

> *Hall County now has more than 200 tractors on the farms, and shipments of new ones are received almost daily. It appears that the big landowners have gone money-mad,*

and, too, at the expense, misery, and suffering of the tenant
farmer, his wife and little children. . . . We believe that there
is sufficient land for all, and . . . that all should have land
upon which to live, rear their families and enjoy the blessings
of home ownership and its happy surroundings. [2]

Even the Farm Security Administration (FSA),
which had been formed to improve life for
sharecroppers and poor farmers, admitted:

[N]othing could prevent the impoverishment of thousands
of farm families, many of whom lost the farms in which they
had invested all their fortunes and hopes. Nothing in the way
of relief could prevent the devastation of millions of acres of
land that had been stripped of its grass cover and skimmed of
its top soil by the high winds. [3]

Much of the soil lay bare. In 1936, news reporter
Ernie Pyle wrote from Kansas, "If you would like to
have your heart broken, just come out here. This is
the dust-storm country. It is the saddest land I have
ever seen."[4]

THE PROMISE OF CALIFORNIA

Few people visited the Dust Bowl states during the
1930s. Visitors were mostly journalists who reported
on the devastation and large California farm growers

who nailed thousands of handbills to trees and telephone poles. The flyers said thousands of workers were needed in California to harvest grapes, peas, peaches, potatoes, carrots, cotton, oranges, beans, and more. The advertisements promised "Plenty of Work!" and "High Wages!" To those in the regions of the Dust Bowl, California offered a promise to solve their problems. Farmers everywhere talked about "goin' to Californ-I-A," where there would be plenty of work. They hoped to earn enough money to

Back in the Dust Bowl

Lawrence Svobida, a Kansas Dust Bowl farmer, chose to stay on the land but wrote a somewhat bleak outlook for the future of the Great Plains in his book, *Farming the Dust Bowl*:

We know that immense areas of land in central China, once cultivated valleys protected by luxuriously clad hills, are now desert, barren and dead. Excavations in the ruins of Babylon reveal to us that the now desert valley of the Euphrates was formerly a rich agricultural region supporting the earliest civilization of which we have any records. There is evidence that much of the great Sahara and Gobi deserts was once fertile. . . . Yet, with all these examples before us, we hesitate to believe that millions of our own acres that have become affected by the same forces of destruction are permanently lost. . . . The Government is making heroic efforts to stop the march of destruction, but, as things stand today, the pessimists have all the best of the argument. They hold the belief that a vast portion of the agricultural areas of the United States is fast heading towards the same fate that overtook these large areas of China and Asia Minor already referred to.[5]

buy a piece of land and build a small house in the middle of an orange grove.

Hundreds of thousands of people decided to go west to California. Great numbers of people left each month, often without telling their neighbors. Lawrence Svobida remembered driving from one vacant house to another, looking for a neighbor who might be home:

> *I drove on, and stopped at the first house I came to. . . . The house was vacant. Most of the roads were blocked by huge dunes of drifted sand, but there was another house about two miles from the first, and I started out in its general direction. . . . This house also had been vacated, though there were signs of recent occupation which told me that the family that had occupied it had only recently pulled up stakes and left.[6]*

Historians estimate 3.5 million people left the Dust Bowl during the 1930s. Approximately 350,000 of these Exodusters, as they were called, headed to California. Others headed to Arizona, Oregon, Washington, and Idaho. Svobida saw it as a tragedy:

> *[A]nd the tragedy of the exodus lies in this, that these are no Argonauts [heroes] setting forth in a spirit of high adventure to pioneer new frontiers, but hordes in despair, haunted by famine and disease, yet fearful of a future without hope.[7]*

*An 80-year-old migrant woman at a refugee camp
in Bakersfield, California*

The Trek West

Most farmers would have preferred to stay in
the Dust Bowl. It was the only home many of them
had ever known. The road west was full of risks and
uncertainties, with no guarantee that life would be
better. But after so many years of hopelessness, they
needed to do something to help their families.

After each devastating dust storm, thousands of
farm families packed up and formed processions

on routes headed west. Some
Exodusters set out on foot with
only a small bundle of personal
items. Others hopped onto
westbound trains. Some traveled
in horse-drawn wagons, but most
packed up a jalopy or an old truck
and crammed in all the material

Car Ownership

In 1936, approximately 50 percent of U.S. families owned cars. In the 1930s, car prices ranged from $550 for a Chevrolet to $5,000 for a Lincoln LeBaron.

possessions it would hold. They built makeshift sides
out of wood slats so they could pile their belongings
even higher. Some even built wooden crates to carry
a goat or cow that could provide milk or meat along
the way. Families packed everything they could into
the truck and hoped their tires would hold up under
the weight of it all. With just a few dollars in their
pockets, they left the plains and headed to their
Promised Land.

The journey was long and difficult. Along the
way, many families were struck by illness and death.
The trip was especially difficult for the very old and
the very young. But families remained hopeful that
their luck would change in California.

The most traveled road west was Route 66, a two-
lane road made of concrete, asphalt, and gravel. The
migrants called it the Mother Road. Some people

stopped along the route to work picking cotton in Texas or lettuce in Arizona. They earned enough money to replenish their supplies of gas and food before continuing west. Some people traveled as long as six months or 2,000 miles (3,219 km) to California.

Route 66 eventually led them out of the plains and through narrow passes of the Rocky Mountains. After passing through Flagstaff, Arizona, they came to the California border at Needles, Arizona.

Route 66

Route 66 (also known as the Main Street of America and the Mother Road) was built in 1926. It originally ran from Chicago, Illinois, and on through Missouri, Kansas, Oklahoma, Texas, New Mexico, Arizona, and California for a total of 2,448 miles (3,940 km). This was the main route for migrants moving west during the Dust Bowl era.

THE CALIFORNIA BORDER

At the border, border guards, often called the "Bum Brigade," met migrating families. These guards did not want more poor "Okies"—a term for migrant workers that was considered offensive at the time—in California. The guards did not like their accents, their gunnysack clothes, or their poverty. They believed migrants would become a burden to the economy. Hundreds of people were turned away if they did not have jobs or cars. They were also turned away if they had bugs—bedbugs, fleas, or boll weevils.

But those who crossed the border celebrated and prepared for the last leg of their trip—150 miles (241 km) through the blistering Mojave Desert, where temperatures topped 120 degrees Fahrenheit (49°C). The migrants traveled the desert at night, hoping their vehicles would make it through the heat. Gas station owner Ralph Richardson remembered the plight of these migrants, whose optimism kept them going:

> *Frightened, those people were frightened, and they came through here thinking they were headed for the Promised Land where they'd say, "Everything's going to be all right." I warned them about those ideas, but they went on.*[8]

As it turned out, Richardson was right—everything would not be all right. California was indeed beautiful, but their dreams of finding work and homes of their own rarely came true.

California orange groves held promise for work for Dust Bowl refugees.

Migrant camp in Bakersfield, California

"Okie, Go Home!"

After enduring the barrenness and heat of the Mojave Desert, the Dust Bowl migrants reached the beautiful Tehachapi Mountains of central California. Migrants wound their way through the mountain range and emerged atop a

2,000-foot (610-m) peak overlooking the lush San
Joaquin Valley. Weary travelers celebrated as they
looked out over their Promised Land.

LOOKING FOR WORK

The road down the Tehachapi Grade dropped
rapidly and dangerously into the southern end
of the huge fertile valley. The worn-out travelers
enthusiastically drove into towns advertised in the
flyers—Bakersfield, Shafter, Delano, and Lamont.
The flyers stated that workers were needed year-
round to pick grapes, dig potatoes, and harvest
lettuce, carrots, and other crops. But celebration
soon turned to disappointment when migrants saw
signs that read, "NO JOBS HERE! IF YOU ARE
LOOKING FOR WORK—KEEP OUT! 10 MEN
FOR EVERY JOB!" Signs in store windows—"NO
OKIES ALLOWED!"—told them they were not
wanted there at all.

There had once been work, but so many Dust
Bowl migrants had come that there were few jobs
available. Large orchard owners were glad there
was an overabundance of workers—they could offer
twenty-five cents or even fifteen cents an hour.
There were too many people desperate for work and

many could not afford to turn down any job despite the low wage. The average income for an Okie family was between $350 and $450 a year. By comparison, the national average salary in the United States was $1,368.

Okies received approximately thirty-five cents an hour picking peaches. A day's wages amounted to about $2.50. When work could be found, they spent 16 hours a day in the fields just to keep their families from starving. But those who had jobs at all were fortunate. Others had to continue traveling in search of farms that might be hiring.

Hopes of ever owning land were dashed. California did not offer land; it offered a few people low-paying jobs on the land. Generally, California farmers were not small family operations. Much of the farmland was owned by large corporations. Landowners hired local managers to supervise the planting and the harvest. Dust Bowl transplants who had dreamed of owning a house and land had little choice but to become migrant farm laborers. They traveled from one huge

Okie to Congressman

Texan Bernice Frederic Sisk was an Exoduster who arrived in the San Joaquin Valley in 1937. He took the first job he could find, thinning nectarines. He was elected to the U.S. House of Representatives in 1954. Sisk served as a Congressman until 1979.

farm operation to another trying to arrive before the thousands of other laborers looking for work. One migrant farmer seeking work near Holtville, California, sat at the edge of a field for weeks, waiting for the crop to mature. The peas froze, however, and the farmer had to wait for the second crop to mature.

Migrants who found work sometimes slept in the fields next to rows of plants so no one could take their spot or their job the next morning. A migrant in Imperial Valley said, "They'll sleep in the row (to hold a place in the field) to earn 60 cents a day."[1]

FROM FARM TO FARM

Traveling from one farm to another meant uprooting the family again and again. Home was not a permanent thing, and temporary living conditions ranged from tolerable to appalling. Children suffered the most, living in squalid conditions by the side of the road in makeshift settlements known as squatter camps, Okievilles, or ditch camps—so named because they were often next to irrigation ditches.

The ditches served as their toilets, and since there was no running water, the opposite side often served as their drinking water. Although state officials sometimes brought in clean drinking water, the Okies still cooked and washed with water from the ditch. Disease was rampant. Cases of cramps, diarrhea, fever, colds, and sore throats were common. Epidemics of dysentery, pneumonia, tuberculosis, polio, whooping cough, meningitis, and other diseases spread throughout the camps.

In the fall of 1936, hundreds of children died from an intestinal flu that caused fever and severe diarrhea. Malnutrition was widespread, and some children died of starvation from a diet of small portions of cabbage, rice, or fried bread. Sometimes all three meals a day consisted of cornbread and beans.

Large farm operations sometimes rented one-room shacks to their migrant workers for about $8 to $10 a month. Each cabin could accommodate four people at most, but it was typically crammed with ten or more. As many as 500 shacks lined the perimeter of some croplands. But when harvest was over, migrant workers had to move on in search of fruit orchards or vegetable crops that were ripe and ready to pick. And they searched for yet another place to live.

Many Californians were unhappy with the number of migrants in the area and would yell insults and, "Okie, go home!" Some Okies did go home, all the way back on Route 66 to their Dust Bowl nightmare that was better than the hellish conditions of the migrant worker. But most of them stayed, unable to afford the long trip back home.

Federal Camps

In 1935, in response to the plight of the Dust Bowl migrants, the Resettlement Administration began building ten federal camps in California to provide emergency shelter and better living conditions

Education for Migrant Children

Migrant children received little education while their families moved from place to place. Many worked in the fields alongside their parents at very young ages. The extra two cents a child made picking a bushel of oranges was sometimes the difference between starving and surviving.

When families stayed in one area long enough, they sometimes sent their children to a public school. But the other children often ridiculed them mercilessly. Most Okie children could not read or write, and people called them stupid. Prejudice against Okies included contempt for the twang and drawl in their talk and for what they wore—usually burlap dresses and overalls with rope straps.

Evelyn Selbach remembered her school days at Vineland School in Bakersfield, California:

I can definitely remember, not appreciating the treatment received at this school. Some of the children at times were made to sit on the floor in the back of the room, even if seats were empty. I believe it was because at times some of these children were barefoot and less clean.[2]

Migrant workers were always on the move, looking for the next harvest.

for the Okies. Where work was abundant, the camps
had permanent buildings. Others could be moved
wherever there was a harvest. Permanent camps
were located in towns such as Marysville, Gridley,
Shafter, Firebaugh, and Lamont. The Arvin Federal
Camp, which opened in 1936, was built between the
towns of Weedpatch and Arvin, about 15 miles (24
km) south of Bakersfield. It was at the base of the
Tehachapi Grade, where Okies had celebrated their
arrival in California.

Earl Shelton was seven years old when his family arrived at Arvin Federal Camp, commonly known as Weedpatch Camp. On and off for 13 years, Earl lived in tent number 529 on a piece of concrete. Later, his family moved to tin cabin number 307. He later recalled the vivid memories of "burning a Sears catalog for light, of hot summer nights cooled only by bedsheets soaked with a hose and then draped over the tent."[3] His father, Tom, was a widower with four sons who had left his home in Scipio, Oklahoma, in a Model A car. The family had traveled with thousands of other Dust Bowl migrants to California in search of work. "I don't recall going hungry," Earl said, "but I know my dad did."[4]

Weedpatch Camp was quite an improvement over ditch camps. The camp housed approximately 300 people. For as little as one dollar a week, or a few hours of work maintaining the camp, people had a place to live. Although their tents or tin cabins often leaked during heavy rains, the people who stayed there were grateful for them.

DiGiorgio Fruit Corporation

Most of the people at Weedpatch Camp worked at the nearby DiGiorgio Fruit Corporation in the San Joaquin Valley. It primarily grew grapes and plums on its 40,000 acres (16,187 ha) of farmland. It was one of the largest farms of its kind in the world. Many migrants survived their California experience by working for Joseph DiGiorgio.

The camps had flush toilets, hot showers, laundry tubs, a medical clinic, a nursery, a place to burn trash, and a community hall for Saturday night dances. Children could buy breakfast for a penny. If someone did not have food, someone else was always willing to share a meal of beans and biscuits. Joe Montgomery remembered what it was like at Weedpatch Camp:

> *Dances were usually held on Saturday night, when the weather permitted, because the dance floor was a wooden floor with no roof. . . . Music was provided by members of the camp. There were fiddlers, harmonica and guitar players. A good time was had by all. The camp members did their own policing and settling of disputes, with Mr. Montgomery [Joe's father] usually acting as bouncer at these Saturday night dances. He was a large man. For Sunday church services, an arbor of brush was erected near the rest rooms.[5]*

Each federal camp had a few employees, but daily operations and social order were delegated to the campers. The camps worked well for those who were able to secure a place in them. But only a few camps had been built; many migrants were still without homes. ⌐

A poor sharecropper's daughter

John Steinbeck

CORRECTING THE OKIE SITUATION

N ewspapers all over the country were reporting on the deplorable conditions of thousands of homeless migrants from the Dust Bowl. John Steinbeck, reporter for the *San Francisco News*, saw firsthand the working and living conditions of the Okies. He talked to the people and listened to their stories about scrounging for food and begging for work. He heard about the handbills that enticed them to California and the details of their journeys on Route 66—of hunger, flat tires, roadside funerals, and stillborn babies.

From his notes, Steinbeck wrote a series of seven newspaper articles in 1936 called *The Harvest Gypsies*. It was published later as a pamphlet titled, *Their Blood is Strong*. In 1939, he wrote *The Grapes of Wrath*. This novel is about the Joads, a family of poor Oklahoma sharecroppers who joined thousands of others in their quest for a better life in California. Although the Joads were fictional, their story showed the struggle of Okies in the 1930s—people driven from their homes by the Great Depression, drought, dust, and tractors. The story also

Pulitzer Prize Winner

In 1940, John Steinbeck was awarded the Pulitzer Prize for *The Grapes of Wrath*. That same year, the book was made into a film, starring Henry Fonda as Tom Joad. The novel was also the basis for Steinbeck receiving the 1962 Nobel Prize for Literature.

showed the strength of the human spirit in difficult circumstances.

For many people across the nation, *The Grapes of Wrath* opened their eyes to a tragedy they knew little about. Others thought Steinbeck had portrayed a negative view of California farmers and capitalism. Some even called the book "communist propaganda" and a "pack of lies."

Depression Photographs

Steinbeck's writing was just one way the nation became aware of the migrants' plight. For five years, photographer Dorothea Lange traveled throughout the Dust Bowl, drove along Route 66, and visited Okievilles and federal camps in California. With her camera, she captured the heart and misery of a displaced people. Much of the time, Lange traveled with economy professor Paul Schuster Taylor, whom she would later marry. Taylor interviewed people and gathered economic information. He hoped his reports would persuade government agencies to improve living conditions for the victims of the Dust Bowl and the Depression.

Lange and Taylor submitted their photos and findings to the government in what was called the

Dorothea Lange's famous photograph, "Migrant Mother"

Taylor-Lange Field Report. It was published in 1939 as *An American Exodus: A Record of Human Erosion.* On April 15, 1938, Taylor spoke to the Commonwealth Club of California, an organization concerned with cultural and public affairs, about the nation's responsibility to aid migrants in California:

> *We cannot stop them from coming by refusing to give them relief in California when they need it. They are forced from their own communities; directly and indirectly we invite them; we use their labor. Not only are they here by tens of thousands of families, but more are coming. . . .*
>
> *We dare not tolerate in our midst their hunger and the malnutrition of their children, their unsanitary living conditions, and their disease. Neither the state of California nor the United States can postpone or avoid this responsibility.*[1]

Taylor and Lange's efforts made some government officials pay attention. Lange's photographs led to her employment with the Farm Security Administration (FSA). Her work as a government photographer helped the nation look at the desolate condition of these people whose futures were so uncertain.

A School for Migrants

Finding a solution to the far-reaching problem of the migrant situation was difficult. But one man tried to make a difference in the lives of one group of Okie children. Leo Hart was a teacher in Bakersfield, California. In 1938, he became head counselor for the Kern County High School District. Students from migrant camps confided in him about the discrimination, the uncertainty, and the hunger that plagued them.

Hart visited the children at Weedpatch Camp. He played tag or

"Migrant Mother"

Dorothea Lange's best-known photograph is called "Migrant Mother." It is one in a series of photographs that Lange took of Florence Owens Thompson and her children. In March 1936, Lange was in Nipomo, California, at the end of a monthlong trip for the Resettlement Administration. Lange, who was drawn to this desperate mother and her children, described her experience:

I do not remember how I explained my presence or my camera to her, but I do remember she asked me no questions. I made five exposures, working closer and closer from the same direction. I did not ask her name or her history. She told me her age, that she was thirty-two. She said that they had been living on frozen vegetables from the surrounding fields, and birds that the children killed. She just sold the tires from her car to buy food. There she sat in that lean-to tent with her children huddled around her, and seemed to know that my pictures might help her, and so she helped me. There was a sort of equality about it.[2]

baseball with them in the vacant field next to the camp. He listened to their Dust Bowl experiences in the windy panhandle and their sufferings along Mother Road.

In 1939, when Hart was elected Kern County superintendent of education, he looked for a way to help the Weedpatch children. "The big problem for me," he said, "was to find out what to do for these children to get them adjusted into society and to take their *rightful place*."[3] He realized it would be a difficult task.

Hart's first plan was to place Okie students in rural outlying schools, but angry parents strongly opposed his idea. They demanded that Okies be completely removed from their public school system. Hart was angered by this attitude. He later said, "I could never understand why they shouldn't be given the same opportunity as

Mob Violence

While Hart made plans to improve Okies' lives, citizens and police were forming armed patrols— Bum Brigades—to guard county borders and keep Okies out. In 1938, an Okie migrant camp located under the Kern River Bridge was burned down. An angry mob was responsible. The same group tried to drive the Okies out of Weedpatch Camp. They arrived at night with pitchforks, guns, bricks, and clubs. Hundreds of Okies who defended themselves were jailed, but no one from the mob was arrested.

others. Someone had to do something for them because no one cared about them."[4]

In April 1940, Hart removed Okie children from the Kern County school district and asked permission to build an emergency school for them. With the help of Dewey Russell, manager of Weedpatch Camp, Hart leased 10 acres (4 ha) next to the camp from the federal government for ten dollars. Hart declared it the Arvin Federal Emergency School—commonly known as Weedpatch School.

In September 1940, Weedpatch School opened. It consisted of two condemned buildings and "fifty poorly clad, undernourished, and skeptical youngsters."[5] Their first lesson was a hands-on course on how to build a school. They laid bricks, nailed boards, put in pipes for running water, and renovated the two condemned buildings. They learned how to plant vegetables, raise livestock, and cook. More traditional classes included history, geography, math, science, chemistry, typing, and sewing.

Students had the opportunity to learn airplane mechanics after their principal, Pete Bancroft, purchased a retired C-46 airplane from the military and parked it at the school. Students were allowed to drive the airplane across the field if their arithmetic grades were 90 percent or above. Another reward for maintaining good grades was the chance to dig in "the hole"—a spot in the ground that would one day become a swimming pool.

Life after Weedpatch School

Many of the migrant children who attended Weedpatch School were successful adults. Willard Melton became a college professor. Joyce Foster became a high school teacher, and Jim Wren became the vice principal at West High School in Bakersfield. Jim Montgomery owned two restaurants in Boise, Idaho, and his brother Bruce became a marketing manager for IBM. Joe Collins became a judge, and Patty Anderson and her sister were teachers in Los Angeles. Others became business owners, legal secretaries, postal clerks, and captains in the fire department.

As the students saw what they could accomplish through determination and hard work at this school, their pride in Weedpatch grew. Approximately 400 students eventually attended the school. Weedpatch student Trice Masters later said:

> The teachers made us feel important and like someone really cared. The school gave us pride and dignity and honor when we didn't have those things. It was our school. It did a great deal to cause us to believe we were special.[6]

Weedpatch School was such a success that by 1944 the people of Kern County were pleading to

have their children enrolled in the Arvin Federal
Emergency School. But the school was forced to
close down that year when its emergency status
expired. The school became part of the Vineland
School District.

A CHANGING ECONOMY

Dust Bowl migrants eventually melded into
the rest of society, largely due to an improving
U.S. economy and a major buildup of the nation's
military. World War II had been brewing since early
1938, when German dictator Adolf Hitler invaded
Austria. For the next three years, the United States
tried to stay out of the war. But when the Japanese
attacked Pearl Harbor, Hawaii, on December 7,
1941, the United States declared war on Japan and
entered World War II. Approximately 16.1 million
armed forces personnel would serve in the war.

Those who did not serve in the war joined a
massive U.S. workforce that scrambled to produce
airplanes, tanks, and antiaircraft weapons. By 1943,
unemployment had dropped to 1.9 percent. The
economy was rebounding. People joined together in
a united effort to win the war and protect the United
States.

The people of the Dust Bowl were healing, and so was the land. Although millions of tons of wind-blown soil would never return to the Great Plains, a variety of factors would make the Dust Bowl livable and productive once again. ⌐

FIRST AID
NURSERY

A nurse cares for migrant children in Arvin, California.

Farmers learned new plowing techniques.

HEALING THE LAND

On July 11, 1938, rain drenched the town of Amarillo, Texas. It was one of many rainfalls that would bring an end to the drought that had afflicted the Dust Bowl since the early 1930s. Franklin Roosevelt was in Amarillo that day; it was one of several stops on his trip through the Dust

Bowl. He addressed the large crowd and the huge band that had gathered to welcome the President of the United States:

> If I had asked the newspapermen on the train what the odds were, they would have given me 100 to 1 that it wouldn't be raining in Amarillo. But it is![1]

The people cheered and were optimistic that more rain would fall that year. Rain did continue to fall, and crops grew. The land began to heal, but it was not the rain alone that restored the damaged soil. For several years, many farmers and government agencies had been working together in a variety of ways to end the dusters that had dumped topsoil across the United States.

Although some farmers resisted federal involvement, many gladly took advantage of government subsidies and new farming methods to control wind erosion, improve the soil, and curb overproduction. About 20 percent of the Dust Bowl region was eventually organized into soil conservation districts in which local farmers implemented new farming and soil-saving techniques.

"A nation that destroys its soil, destroys itself."[2]

—*President Franklin Roosevelt*

Congress had established the Shelterbelt Project in 1934. It was one of the first large-scale programs to preserve the Great Plains. In March 1935, workers began planting long rows of native trees from North Dakota to Texas in order to protect the land from wind and drought. The U.S. Forest Service hired locals to plant and nurture 1,000 miles (1,609 km) of 220 million trees.

Dusters Return

In the 1940s, wheat, cotton, and beef were especially in high demand due to World War II, and prices went up. New farmers wanted a "piece of the pie" and moved into the Dust Bowl, often working much of the submarginal land that had been abandoned in the 1930s. Some farmers warned that another Dust Bowl was in the making, but few paid attention. From 1941 to 1950, millions of acres of land were plowed and planted. By 1947, the Great Plains again experienced dust storms and a decrease in rainfall.

In addition, government programs encouraged farmers to reduce the amount of land they cultivated. The federal government purchased land that was submarginal—not good farmland. They reseeded it with native prairie grasses, the original ground cover that had protected the soil from erosion for centuries. Much of this restored land was designated as National Grasslands.

NEW FARMING METHODS

The government also paid farmers to implement innovative farm practices. The Soil

Workers plant a strip of trees to shield the land from wind.

Conservation Service taught farmers to plow rough furrows—shallow trenches in the ground—that followed the curves of the land and trapped moisture and topsoil in their ridges. LeRoy Hoffman remembered learning to change the way he plowed so the rainwater "wouldn't just come running clear down that hill."[3]

Farmers also learned strip cropping. This is a method of planting a variety of crops such as wheat, corn, and sorghum next to each other in strips. Between each type of crop, farmers grew grass and hay, which had strong, dense root systems that absorbed the rain and held back runoff. Grass and hay also slowed down the dust that was picked up by the ever-present winds and prevented drifts and dusters from developing.

Terracing—planting on different levels in a stair-step fashion—was implemented to prevent rainwater from washing away down a slope. Farmers also learned to leave the stubble in the ground after harvest and wait until spring to plow. This provided ground cover during the winter months.

Responding to Nature

In 1949, the Great Plains was hit again with drought and what some would call a "new Dust Bowl." During the 1940s, farmers had planted millions of acres in grain and other crops to meet the high demand for food during World War II, which lasted until 1945. With the droughts from 1949 through 1957, erosion dust storms returned.

The dusters never reached the magnitude of those in the 1930s, but farmers again had to put conservation methods into practice in order to restore the damaged soil. The land was restored in much less time than during the 1930s.

To control the recurring drought problem in the Great Plains, beginning in the 1950s, many farmers turned to irrigation. They pumped water from aquifers, or underground flows of water, into large sprinkler systems that regularly watered their crops. A major source of this underground water is the Ogallala Aquifer. It lies underneath about 225,000 square miles (582,747 sq km) of the Great Plains, under parts of Nebraska, Kansas, Colorado, Wyoming, South Dakota, Oklahoma, Texas, and New Mexico. Heavy pumping from the aquifer has led to lower water levels. When the rate of use exceeds the rate of water replenishment, an aquifer can eventually dry up.

Not all farmers cooperated with the government. Some remained independent and would not accept federal help. Others disagreed with the new farming practices, especially the reduction of crops to force prices up. Tenant farmers who rented land were especially hurt by the federal subsidies program, which gave financial aid only to landowners. Many tenant farmers were forced to abandon farms and find other places to live and work. Fortunately, the law was later amended to include tenant farmers.

By 1937, new farming methods were starting to pay off, and the land was beginning to heal. The land was now soaking up more water and resisting erosion. Rainfall had returned to normal by 1939. Throughout the 1940s, the Great Plains received more than the average rainfall. Crops were nourished, the soil grew strong, and dust storms abated. For all practical purposes, the Dust Bowl was over. Drought and dust storms would still be a part of the Great Plains, as they always had, but not as fiercely as they had during the Dirty Thirties.

CHANGED FOREVER

The Dust Bowl left its mark on the land, and it also changed a large group of people. Even though the land and the economy had improved after World War II, poor health and painful memories clung to Dust Bowlers for the rest of their lives. Many had respiratory illnesses from the dust they had once inhaled. For most, the memories of unemployment, starvation, discrimination, homelessness, and shattered dreams never faded. Lawrence Svobida recalled:

> *My dreams and ambitions had been flouted by nature, and my shattered ideals seemed gone forever. The very desire to make a success of my life was gone; the spirit and urge to strive were dead within me. Fate had dealt me a cruel blow above which I felt utterly unable to rise.*[4]

But neither the cruel blow of the Dust Bowl nor the undying memories would destroy those who lived through it. Their extremely difficult circumstances made them a strong, determined, and dependable people who eventually took back their rightful places in society and made the nation a better place. These people left their mark on the nation. Future generations can learn from their mistakes and inherit their courage.

Mr. and Mrs. Hall stand on the porch of their new home after completing
a training program given by the Farm Security Administration.

TIMELINE

1803	1862	1870s
The United States purchases the Louisiana Territory from France.	President Abraham Lincoln signs the Homestead Act on May 20, granting free land in the Great Plains.	The U.S. government begins to move Native Americans to reservations to make room for new settlers.

1930s	1932	1933
Drought plagues the Great Plains states throughout the decade.	Members of the Iowa Farmers' Holiday Association call a strike on July 4.	Franklin Roosevelt is inaugurated as president of the United States on March 4; Congress begins passing New Deal legislation.

1889

A huge land rush establishes two Oklahoma cities—Guthrie and Oklahoma City—in one day on April 22.

1914

World War I begins, increasing the need for wheat production.

1929

The stock market crashes on Black Tuesday, October 29.

1933

Congress passes the Agricultural Adjustment Act on May 12.

1934

On May 11, a 36-hour dust storm covers 1,500 miles (2,414 km) and dumps dirt on cities all the way to the East Coast.

1935

A dust storm destroys 5 million acres (2 million ha) of wheat in Great Plains states on March 15.

TIMELINE

1935	1935	1935
In March, trees are planted from North Dakota to Texas as part of the Shelterbelt Project.	The largest dust storm yet hits the Great Plains on April 14, Black Sunday.	President Roosevelt establishes the Resettlement Administration on April 30.

1939	1940	1940
John Steinbeck writes *The Grapes of Wrath*, a novel about the plight of Dust Bowl migrants.	In April, Leo B. Hart leases land to build the Arvin Federal Emergency School.	Weedpatch School opens in September with 50 migrant students.

1935

Dust Bowlers begin leaving their farms and heading west.

1935

Dorothea Lange and Paul Schuster Taylor submit their Taylor-Lange Field Report to the government.

1936

The Arvin Federal Camp opens south of Bakersfield, California, in January.

1941

Japan bombs Pearl Harbor, Hawaii, on December 7; the United States enters World War II.

1943

Most Americans are employed, and Dust Bowlers have become part of regular society.

1949

A "new Dust Bowl" hits the Great Plains states after drought and excessive tilling of the land.

ESSENTIAL FACTS

DATE OF EVENT

1931 to 1943

PLACE OF EVENT

The Great Plains

KEY PLAYERS

❖ Great Plains farmers

❖ Herbert Hoover

❖ Franklin D. Roosevelt

❖ John Steinbeck

❖ Dorothea Lange

❖ Leo B. Hart

HIGHLIGHTS OF EVENT

❖ Great Plains farmers responded to the increased demand for wheat during World War I (1914–1918), which resulted in the land being overfarmed.

❖ Drought plagued the Great Plains states from 1931 to 1940.

❖ The Iowa Farmers Holiday Association strike began on July 4, 1932, to demand higher prices for their crops.

❖ Franklin D. Roosevelt was inaugurated as president of the United States on March 4, 1933. Congress began to pass New Deal legislation.

❖ Congress passed the Agricultural Adjustment Act on May 12, 1933, to pay farmers not to plant crops on their land.

- On May 11, 1934, a 36-hour dust storm covered 1,500 miles (2,414 km), and dumped 12 million tons (11 million t) of dirt on cities all the way to the East Coast.

- On March 15, 1935, a dust storm destroyed 5 million acres (2 million ha) of wheat in Great Plains states.

- On April 14, 1935, the largest dust storm yet hit the Great Plains on Black Sunday.

- On April 30, 1935, President Roosevelt established the Resettlement Administration (later called the Farm Security Administration), which provided government funds to resettle farmers living on submarginal land to more productive farm areas.

- From 1935 to 1941, Dust Bowl farmers left the plains and migrated west.

- On December 7, 1941, Japan bombed Pearl Harbor, Hawaii, and the United States entered World War II. The war increased jobs and brought an end to the Great Depression.

Quote

"The impact is like a shovelful of fine sand flung against the face. People caught in their own yards grope for the doorstep. Cars come to a standstill, for no light in the world can penetrate that swirling murk. . . . We live with the dust, eat it, sleep with it, watch it strip us of possessions and the hope of possessions." —*Avis Carlson*, The New Republic

ADDITIONAL RESOURCES

SELECT BIBLIOGRAPHY

Henderson, Caroline. *Letters from the Dust Bowl*. Ed. Alvin O. Turner. Norman, OK: University of Oklahoma Press, 2001.

Henshaw, Betty Grant. *Children of the Dust: An Okie Family Story*. Ed. Sandra Scofield. Lubbock, TX: Texas Tech University Press, 2006.

La Chapelle, Peter. *Proud to Be an Okie: Cultural Politics, Country Music, and Migration to Southern California*. Berkeley, CA: University of California Press, 2007.

Low, Ann Marie. *Dust Bowl Diary*. Lincoln, NE: University of Nebraska Press, 1984.

Riney-Kehrberg, Pamela. *Rooted in Dust: Surviving Drought and Depression in Southern Kansas*. Lawrence, KS: University Press of Kansas, 1994.

Steinbeck, John. *The Grapes of Wrath*. New York: Penguin Books, 2002.

Svobida, Lawrence. *Farming the Dust Bowl: A First-Hand Account from Kansas*. Lawrence, KS: University Press of Kansas, 1986.

FURTHER READING

Cooper, Michael L. *Dust to Eat: Drought and Depression in the 1930s*. New York: Clarion Books, 2001.

Freedman, Russell. *Children of the Great Depression*. New York: Clarion Books, 2005.

Meltzer, Milton. *Driven from the Land: The Story of the Dust Bowl*. New York: Benchmark Books, 2000.

Press, Petra. *A Cultural History of the United States through the Decades: The 1930s*. San Diego, CA: Lucent Books, 1999.

Stanley, Jerry. *Children of the Dust Bowl: The True Story of the School at Weedpatch Camp*. New York: Crown Publishers, 1992.

Yancey, Diane. *Life During the Dust Bowl*. San Diego, CA: Thomson Gale. 2004.

Web Links

To learn more about the Dust Bowl, visit ABDO Publishing Company online at **www.abdopublishing.com**. Web sites about the Dust Bowl are featured on our Book Links page. These links are routinely monitored and updated to provide the most current information available.

Places To Visit

Franklin D. Roosevelt Presidential Library and Museum
4079 Albany Post Road
Hyde Park, NY 12538
845-486-7770
www.fdrlibrary.marist.edu
Features exhibits on the Great Depression and the Dust Bowl.

Kansas Museum of History
6425 Southwest Sixth Avenue
Topeka, KS 66615
785-272-8681
www.kshs.org/places/museum.htm
Displays art and artifacts from the Dust Bowl era and gives detailed accounts of the 1930s and life during the Dust Bowl.

Sunset Camp
8305 Sunset Boulevard
Bakersfield, CA 93307
661-832-1299
www.nationalregisterofhistoricplaces.com/ca/Kern/state.html
Sunset Camp was originally known as Arvin Federal Government Camp or Weedpatch Camp. The camp exists today and is still used by migrant workers. A Dust Bowl Festival is held there annually.

Glossary

black blizzard
A large dust storm with very low visibility.

commodity
A product of agriculture or mining that is shipped to market.

drought
A long period of abnormally low rainfall.

duster
A dust storm.

exodus
A mass migration of people.

furrow
A long, narrow, shallow trench made in the ground by a plow.

gale
A very strong wind.

Great Plains
Area of the United States and Canada characterized by prairie and steppe.

homestead
Area of land in the West granted by the U.S. government to individuals willing to live and farm the land for five years.

jalopy
An old, worn-out vehicle.

locust
An insect that often migrates in immense swarms and devours vegetation and crops.

migrant
A worker who travels from one area to another in search of jobs.

prairie
> A large area of open grassland.

shanty
> A roughly built, often ramshackle shack.

snuster
> A dust storm that has mixed with snow.

sorghum
> Varieties of grass cultivated as grain or as a source of syrup.

steppe
> A vast semiarid, grass-covered plain.

stock
> A fund that a corporation raises through the sale of shares.

stubble
> Short, stiff stalks of grain or hay remaining in a field after harvest.

subsidy
> Financial assistance granted by a government.

terrace
> To form a hillside or slope into steplike levels.

thresh
> To beat the stems and husks of grain with a machine in order to separate the grain from the straw.

till
> To prepare land for growing crops by plowing.

SOURCE NOTES

Chapter 1. Black Sunday

1. R. Douglas Hurt. *The Dust Bowl: An Agricultural and Social History.* Chicago: Nelson-Hall, 1981. 1.
2. John Steinbeck. *Grapes of Wrath.* New York: Penguin Books, 2002.
3. Donald Worster. *Dust Bowl: The Southern Plains in the 1930s.* Oxford: Oxford University Press, 1979. 28.
4. "Surviving the Dust Bowl: Black Sunday (April 14, 1935)." PBS. 24 Sept. 2007. <http://www.pbs.org/wgbh/amex/dustbowl/peopleevents/pandeAMEX07.html>.

Chapter 2. Prelude to Disaster

1. R. Douglas Hurt. *The Dust Bowl: An Agricultural and Social History.* Chicago: Nelson-Hall, 1981. 4–5.
2. Ibid. 5.
3. *Harper's Weekly* 33 (May 18, 1889): 391-394. William Willard Howard. "The Rush to Oklahoma." 2 Oct. 2007. <http://www.library.cornell.edu/Reps/DOCS/landrush.htm>.
4. "Program Description." *Surviving the Dust Bowl* [film transcript]. PBS Online. 17 Oct. 2007. <http://www.pbs.org/wgbh/amex/dustbowl/filmmore/description.html>.

Chapter 3. Depression and Drought

1. Ann Marie Low. *Dust Bowl Diary.* Lincoln, NB: University of Nebraska Press, 1984. 33.
2. Ibid. 49.
3. Lawrence Svobida. *Farming the Dust Bowl.* Lawrence, KS: University Press of Kansas, 1986. 62.

Chapter 4. Farmers Fight Back

1. Milton Meltzer. *Brother, Can You Spare a Dime? The Great Depression 1929–1933.* New York: Facts on File, 1991. 87.
2. "This Land Is Your Land." Woody Guthrie Lyrics. Jan. 2008. <http://www.woodyguthrie.org/Lyrics/This_Land.htm>.
3. William H. Hull. *The Dirty Thirties.* Edina, MN: William H. Hull, 1989. 135.

4. "Great Depression and World War II, 1929-1945: President Franklin Delano Roosevelt and the New Deal." The Library of Congress. 24 Oct. 2007. <http://memory.loc.gov/learn/features/timeline/depwwii/newdeal/newdeal.html>.
5. "Woody Guthrie Biography." Woody Guthrie. 23 Oct. 2007. <http://www.woodyguthrie.org/biography/biography4.htm>.

Chapter 5. Dusters, Snusters, and Black Blizzards
1. "Enhanced Transcript." *Surviving the Dust Bowl* [film transcript]. PBS Online. 17 Oct. 2007. <http://www.pbs.org/wgbh/amex/dustbowl/filmmore/transcript/index.html>.
2. Ibid.
3. T.H. Watkins. *The Great Depression: America in the 1930s*. Boston, MA: Little Brown and Co., 1993. 191.
4. Ann Marie Low. *Dust Bowl Diary*. Lincoln, NB: University of Nebraska Press, 1984, 95.
5. "Dust Pneumonia Blues." Woody Guthrie. 24 Oct. 2007. <http://www.woodyguthrie.org/Lyrics?Dust_Pneumonia_Blues.htm>.
6. John R. Wunder, Frances W. Kaye, and Vernon Carstensen, eds. *Americans View Their Dust Bowl Experience*. Niwot, CO: University Press of Colorado, 1999. 164.
7. "Imogene Glover on: saying Good-bye." Film transcript of *Surviving the Dust Bowl*. PBS Online. 17 Oct. 2007. <http://www.pbs.org/wgbh/amex/dustbowl/filmmore/reference/interview/glover06.html>.
8. R. Douglas Hurt. *The Dust Bowl: An Agricultural and Social History*. Chicago: Nelson-Hall, 1981. 58.
9. Ibid. 59.
10. "Program Description." *Surviving the Dust Bowl* [film transcript]. PBS Online. 17 Oct. 2007. <http://www.pbs.org/wgbh/amex/dustbowl/filmmore/description.html>.
11. Lawrence Svobida. *Farming the Dust Bowl*. Lawrence, KS: University Press of Kansas, 1986. 238.

Source Notes Continued

Chapter 6. Exodusters
1. Lawrence Svobida. *Farming the Dust Bowl*. Lawrence, KS: University Press of Kansas, 1986. 206.
2. Dorothea Lange and Paul Schuster Taylor. *An American Exodus: A Record of Human Erosion*. New York: Reynal & Hitchcock, 1939. 87.
3. Lawrence Svobida. *Farming the Dust Bowl*. Lawrence, KS: University Press of Kansas, 1986. 239–240.
4. "The Drought." *Surviving the Dust Bowl* [film transcript]. 17 Oct. 2007. <http://www.pbs.org/wgbh/amex/dustbowl/peopleevents/pandeAMEX06.html>.
5. Lawrence Svobida. *Farming the Dust Bowl*. Lawrence, KS: University Press of Kansas, 1986. 145–146.
6. Ibid. 210–215.
7. Ibid. 240.
8. T.H. Watkins. *The Hungry Years: A Narrative History of the Great Depression in America*. New York: Holt, 2000. 436.

Chapter 7. "Okie, Go Home!"
1. Dorothea Lange and Paul Schuster Taylor. *An American Exodus: A Record of Human Erosion*. New York: Reynal & Hitchcock, 1939. 115.
2. Selbach Johnson and Evelyn Ruth. "Weedpatch Camp (Arvin Federal Government Camp): Personal Reminiscences of the Selbach Family." *The Arvin Tiller/Lamont* Report Supplement, October 20, 1999. Weedpatch Camp. 19 Oct. 2007. <http://www.weedpatchcamp.com/Reminiscences/Selbach.htm>.
3. Patricia Leigh Brown. "Oklahomans Try to Save Their California Culture." *The New York Times*. 5 Feb. 2002. 24 Oct. 2007. <http://www.weedpatchcamp.com/Newspaper%20Articles/NY_times.htm>.
4. Ibid.
5. Joe Montgomery. "Weedpatch Camp (Arvin Federal Government Camp): Personal Reminiscences of the Montgomery Family." *The Arvin Tiller/Lamont Reporter*. Weedpatch Camp. 19 Oct. 2007. <http://www.weedpatchcamp.com/Reminiscences/Montgomery.htm>.

Chapter 8. Correcting the Okie Situation
1. Paul S. Taylor. "What Shall We Do with Them?" Address to the Commonwealth Club of California, April 15, 1938. Paul S. Taylor. *On the Ground in the Thirties*. Salt Lake City, UT: 1983. 208–209.
2. "Dorothea Lange's 'Migrant Mother' Photographs in the Farm Security Administration Collection: An Overview." Library of Congress. 23 Oct. 2007. <http://www.loc.gov/rr/print/list/128_migm.html>.
3. Jerry Stanley. *Children of the Dust Bowl: The True Story of the School at Weedpatch Camp*. New York: Crown Publishers, 1992. 41.
4. Ibid. 44.
5. Ibid. 45.
6. Ibid. 69.

Chapter 9. Healing the Land
1. "Address at Ellwood Park, Amarillo, Texas. July 11th, 1938." The American Presidency Project. 22 Oct. 2007. <http://www.presidency.ucsb.edu/ws/index.php?pid=15678>.
2. "Desertification: Earth's Silent Scourge." International Information Programs. USinfo.state.gov Web site. 23 Oct. 2007. <http://usinfo.state.gov/products/pubs/desertific/experience.htm>.
3. "Farming in the 1930s." Wessels Living History Farm. 22 Oct. 2007. <http://www.livinghistoryfarm.org/farminginthe30s/crops_11.html>.
4. "Surviving the Dust Bowl" [film]. PBS Online. 22 Oct. 2007. <http://www.pbs.org/wgbh/amex/dustbowl/sfeature/eyewitness.html>.

Index

Agricultural Adjustment Act, 36–37, 38
Agricultural Adjustment Administration, 36
Arvin Federal Camp, 72–74, 81–82
Arvin Federal Emergency School, 83–85

Black Sunday, 6–12, 52
Boston, Massachusetts, 44, 51
Brown, Wanita, 52
"Bum Brigade," 63, 82

California
advertisements, 59, 67
migration to, 59–64, 66
orchards, 67, 70
promise of, 59–60, 67, 70
Chicago, Illinois, 12, 44, 51, 63
Civilian Conservation Corps, 39–40

DiGiorgio Fruit Corporation, 73
Dust Bowl
drought, 7, 9, 12, 15, 21, 22, 27–28, 49, 56–57, 77, 88, 90, 92, 93
health effects, 48, 49, 94
heat, 15, 27–29, 57
life in, 42–54, 59
location, 11
optimism, 7, 52–53, 64, 89
dust storm
animals, 7, 28, 44, 48
black blizzard, 8–10, 44–47, 49, 53, 57
cleanup, 10–12, 47–48
damage, 12, 40, 48, 57
deaths, 49, 50

duster, 8, 9, 10, 29, 42–43, 45, 47, 51–52, 89, 90, 92
electric charge, 43
snuster, 12, 44
visibility, 10, 40, 43–44, 45, 50, 51
wind speeds, 8, 30, 49

Exoduster, 60, 62, 68

Farm Security Administration, 39, 58, 80
farmer protests, 30, 32–33
farming practices
equipment, 20–21, 34, 36, 44, 57
irrigation, 9, 92
overfarming, 22
plowing, 20, 28, 91, 92
strip cropping, 91
terracing, 92
foreclosures, 34, 57

Glover, Imogene, 52–53
Grapes of Wrath, The, 10, 77–78
Great Depression, 22, 25, 26, 36, 39, 56, 77, 78
homeless, 38–39, 94
unemployment, 26, 38, 85, 94
Great Plains
climate, 14–15, 17
history of, 16–17
prairie grasses, 15, 22, 58, 90, 91–92
settlements, 18–20
Guthrie, Woody, 35, 50

hailstorms, 26, 27, 29
Hart, Leo, 81–83
Hoover, Herbert, 26, 39

Iowa Farmers Union, 33

land runs, 18
Lange, Dorothea, 78–80, 81
Louisiana Purchase, 16, 17
Low, Ann Marie, 25–26,
  27–28, 49–50

McCarty, John, 53
migrant farmers
  competition for jobs, 67–69
  disease, 70
  federal camps, 71–72, 74. *See
    also* Arvin Federal Camp.
  pay, 68
  squatter camps, 69–71
  working conditions, 68–69
"Migrant Mother," 79, 81
Mississippi River, 16
Mojave Desert, 64, 66

National Grasslands, 90
Native Americans, 16
New Deal, 37, 39–40
New York, 12, 38, 51

"Okies," 63, 67–74, 76–78
  California border, 63–64
  children, 69–70, 71, 73, 74,
    81–84
  discrimination, 67, 71,
    81–83, 94

penny auctions, 35, 36

Reno, Milo, 33
Resettlement Administration,
  39, 71, 81
Roosevelt, Franklin, 36, 37–38,
  39, 88–89
Route 66, 62–63, 71, 77, 78

San Joaquin Valley, 67, 68, 73
Shelterbelt Project, 90
Soil Conservation Service,
  90–91
Steinbeck, John, 10, 76–78
stock market crash of 1929,
  24–25
suitcase farmers, 21
Svobida, Lawrence, 29, 54, 56,
  59, 60, 94

Taylor, Paul Schuster, 78, 80
Taylor-Lange Field Report, 80
tenant farmers, 57, 58, 93

Weedpatch Camp. *See* Arvin
  Federal Camp
Weedpatch School. *See* Arvin
  Federal Emergency School
Wells, Helen, 6
Wells, Rolley, 7
wheat, 20–22, 26–28, 29, 33,
  34, 56–57, 90, 91
Works Progress Administration,
  40
World War I, 20
World War II, 26, 85, 90, 92,
  94

About the Author

Sue Vander Hook has been writing and editing books for more than 15 years. Although her writing career began with several nonfiction books for adults, Vander Hook's main focus is educational books for children and young adults. She especially enjoys writing about historical events and biographies of people who made a difference. Her published works also include a high school curriculum and several series on disease, technology, and sports. She lives with her family in Minnesota.

Photo Credits

AP Images, cover, 6, 11, 19, 24, 37, 41, 42, 45, 61, 66, 72, 76, 87, 88, 91, 95; Red Line Editorial, 13; Solomon D. Butcher/ AP Images, 14; Image Source/AP Images, 23; John Gaps III/ AP Images, 31; Cliff Schiappa/Stringer/Getty Images, 32; Alfred Eisenstaedt/Stringer/Time & Life Pictures/Getty Images, 46; FSA/ Staff/Getty Images, 55; Dorothea Lange/Stringer/Time & Life Pictures/Getty Images, 56; Brakefield Photo/AP Images, 65; James N. Keen/AP Images, 75; Dorothea Lange/AP Images, 79